RANDY
MOSS

RANDY
MOSS

BOB TEMPLE

THE CHILD'S WORLD®, INC.

ON THE COVER...

Front cover: Randy concentrates as he runs during a game against the New England Patriots on September 17, 2000.
Page 2: Randy runs the ball during the NFC Championship game against the Atlanta Falcons on January 17, 2000.

Published in the United States of America by The Child's World®, Inc.
PO Box 326
Chanhassen, MN 55317-0326
800-599-READ
www.childsworld.com

Product Manager Mary Berendes
Editor Katherine Stevenson
Designer Mary Berendes

Photo Credits
© AFP/CORBIS: 2, 6, 9, 15, 16
© AP/WideWorld Photos: 10, 19, 23
© Reuters NewMedia Inc./CORBIS: 20
© Rob Tringali/SportsChrome-USA: cover
© Vincent Manniello/SportsChrome-USA: 13

Library of Congress Cataloging-in-Publication Data
Temple, Bob.
Randy Moss / by Bob Temple.
p. cm.
Includes index.
ISBN 1-56766-968-9
1. Moss, Randy—Juvenile literature.
2. Football players—United States—Biography—Juvenile literature.
[1. Moss, Randy. 2. Football players. 3. Afro-Americans—Biography.] I. Title.
GV939.M67 T46 2001
796.332'092—dc21
00-011885

TABLE OF CONTENTS

HIGH-FLYING ACT

Vikings **Wide receiver** Randy Moss streaks down the sideline. The other team's **defensive back** is just behind him. Another defensive back rushes over to help his teammate. It looks as if Randy is covered on this play.

But it doesn't matter. The **quarterback** reaches back and lofts the ball toward the end zone—in Randy's direction—even though Randy has two players covering him. It looks like trouble for the Vikings. As the ball comes toward the three players, Randy jumps and rises above the two defenders. He snatches the ball out of the air and lands in the end zone as the two opponents fall to the ground. It's a **touchdown!**

That's the kind of football player Randy Moss is. Just when it seems as though he can't possibly make the catch, he figures out a way to do it. That's what has made Randy one of the best players in the National Football League.

STANDING OUT EARLY

Randy was born on February 13, 1977, in Rand, West Virginia. His mother, Maxine, was a single parent who worked long hours to earn enough money to support the family. She made sure that Randy grew up with values. He attended church three times a week as a child.

 Randy catches a touchdown pass in front of an Arizona Cardinals player in the NFC Divisional playoff game on January 10, 2000.

Randy never lived with his father, but he looked up to his half-brother, Eric, who was two years older. Eric was a very good athlete, and Randy helped him by carrying his equipment to games and practices. Soon, Randy blossomed into a good athlete in his own right.

From an early age, Randy dreamed about being a **professional** athlete. Part of the reason was that his mother worked so hard. Randy wanted to be able to make enough money so she wouldn't have to work any more.

HIGH SCHOOL HIGHS AND LOWS

In the fall of 1991, Randy enrolled at DuPont High School in Belle, West Virginia. High school was a difficult time for Randy, because most of the students in the school were white, and Randy is black. Some of the white students didn't like him because of the color of his skin. They threatened him, called him names, and worse. Randy was forced to battle this type of **racism** all through high school.

In sports, Randy had few problems. The DuPont football team won the 1994 West Virginia state championship, and Randy was named the state's Football Player of the Year. He was also named the state's top basketball player two years in a row.

Randy tries to get by Detroit Lion Bryant Westbrook after catching a pass on January 2, 2000.

All of the top colleges in the country wanted Randy to come play for them. People in West Virginia wanted him to play at the University of West Virginia, but Randy decided to branch out. He accepted a **scholarship** to Notre Dame, one of the top football programs in the nation. His dreams were coming true.

Randy tried his best to stay out of trouble, but trouble often found him. One day, a friend of Randy's got into a fight at school. Randy jumped in to help his friend. It was a big mistake. The police were called, and Randy was arrested. Suddenly, his dreams were slipping away. DuPont High School expelled Randy, and Notre Dame cancelled his scholarship. Even worse, Randy had to spend 30 days in jail.

ANOTHER CHANCE

Notre Dame's coach was Lou Holtz. Even though Notre Dame cancelled Randy's scholarship, Coach Holtz still believed in the young player. He called his friend, Bobby Bowden, coach of the powerful Florida State University team. Coach Bowden invited Randy to come to Florida State. He said that if Randy would agree to sit out a year, he could play.

Randy runs past New Orleans Saints defensive back Chris Oldham on August 5, 2000.

Randy agreed, but he never got the chance to play for Florida State. He participated in spring practice there in 1996 and returned home to West Virginia for the summer. All Randy had to do was to stay out of trouble and he would be able to play for one of the top programs in the country. But he made another mistake. He tried drugs. When the police caught him, he was sent back to jail for 90 days. And Coach Bowden cancelled Randy's scholarship at Florida State. "Jail was the lowest," Randy said later. "Jail was a place where you get your mind right."

A FRESH START

Randy wondered whether he had blown his chance to become a professional football player. He wanted one more chance. He found it at Marshall University, a smaller college in West Virginia. Bob Pruett, an assistant at Florida State when Randy was there, was the new head coach at Marshall. Pruett told Randy he could come and play at Marshall, but that it would be his last chance. That was all Randy needed to hear.

Marshall played in Division 1-AA, a league for smaller schools. By the end of his freshman season in 1996, Randy had already made his mark as one of the best players in Division 1-AA history. During the regular season, Randy caught 19 touchdown passes, a new record for college freshmen.

Randy makes a quick turn to dodge players from the Chicago Bears on November 14, 1999.

Randy wasn't done. In Division 1-AA, the national championship is decided by playoffs rather than bowl games. Thanks to Randy, Marshall's Thundering Herd was one of the top teams. Randy kept scoring touchdowns, and Marshall kept winning games. In the national championship game against Montana, Randy caught nine passes for 220 yards and 4 touchdowns, leading the Thundering Herd to the national championship. Randy finished his freshman season with 28 touchdown catches, tying the Division 1-AA record held by the great Jerry Rice.

MOVING UP

The next season, Marshall moved up to play in Division 1, competing with the nation's bigger schools. That meant playing against much better teams. Randy wasn't worried. In fact, he thought it was good news. He would have a chance to prove that he was one of the best players in the country. Once he had done that, he felt, he would be ready to leave college and go to the NFL.

Randy's first Division 1 game was against West Virginia, the school many people had wanted Randy to attend in the first place. He was spectacular despite being covered by two players for most of the game. He scored two touchdowns and caught seven passes. Randy was on his way.

Randy jumps high above two Green Bay Packers to catch a pass for a first down on November 22, 2000.

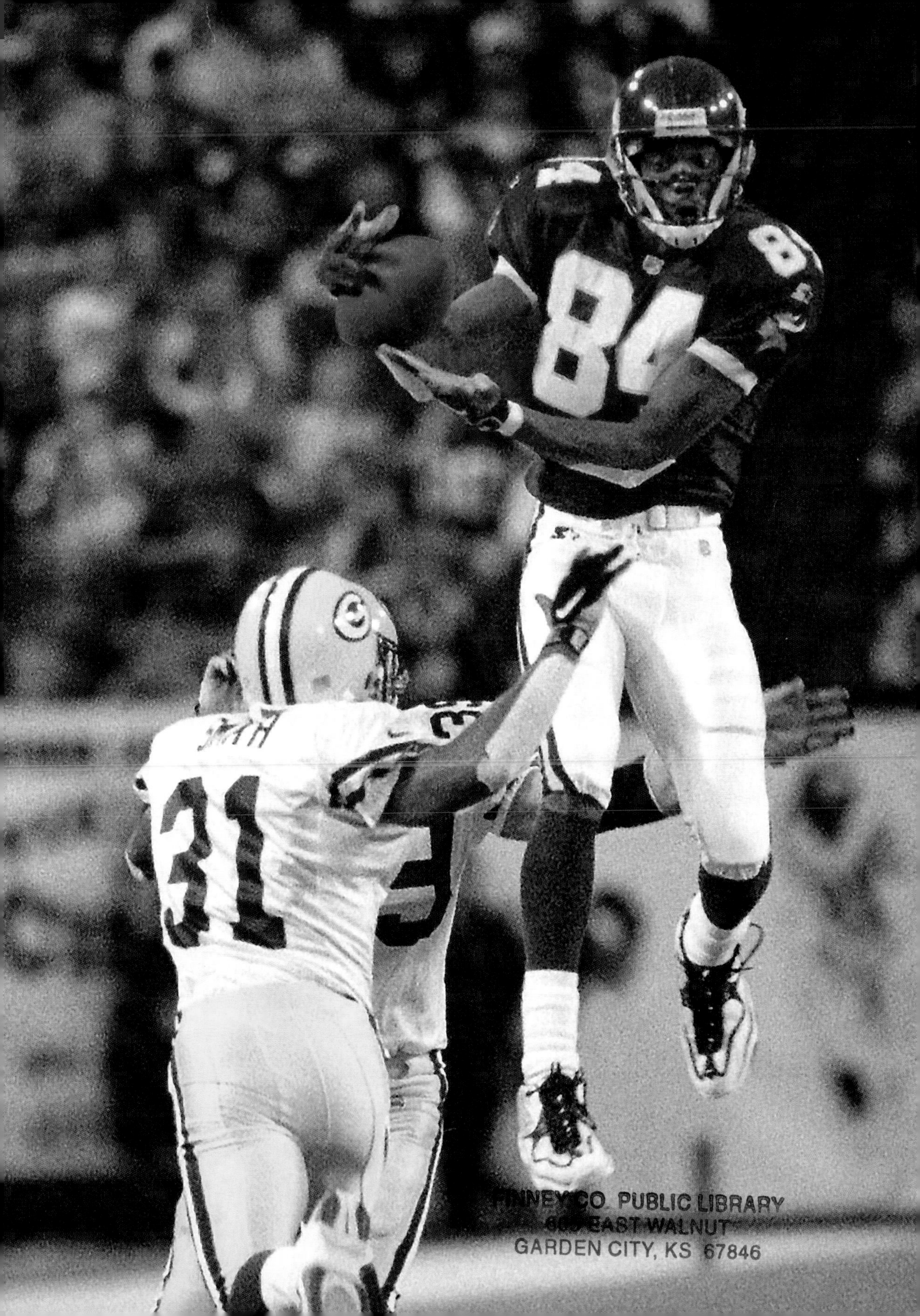

By the time the season ended, Randy had caught 25 touchdown passes to set a new Division 1 record. He won the Biletnikoff Award as the nation's best receiver. He also finished fourth in the voting for the Heisman Trophy, the award given to the best college football player in the country. He was also a first-team All-American for the second year in a row.

ON TO THE PROS

Randy knew he was ready for NFL **draft.** The question was whether the NFL was ready for him. Most NFL teams knew he could be a great player, but some worried about his past troubles. When it came time for the draft, many teams passed him by, choosing players who had never been in trouble.

It wasn't until the 21st pick of the draft that Randy was chosen by the Minnesota Vikings. The Vikings felt that Randy's desire to play football would keep him out of trouble. It also helped that Randy's half-brother, Eric, was already a member of the Vikings! When Randy joined the Vikings, he had one thing in mind—proving that the Vikings had made the right choice. It didn't take him very long.

Randy makes a catch in front of an Arizona Cardinals player during the NFC Divisional playoff game on January 10, 2000.

A ROLE MODEL

Randy had a big advantage in coming to the Vikings—his new teammate, Cris Carter. Cris is one of the best receivers in the history of the NFL, but he also had some troubles in his past. He knew from experience how to turn a life around. Right away, Cris took Randy under his wing.

During the off-season, Cris stays in shape by **training** near his home in Florida. He invited Randy to come and work out with him, and Randy went. Working with Cris helped Randy understand what it would take to be an NFL star. It helped him with his game, and it helped him off the field, too.

ROOKIE SENSATION

In his first NFL game in 1998, Randy caught his first pass on the Vikings' third play. His next catch was a 48-yard touchdown pass from Brad Johnson. Randy was on his way! Soon he was making headlines all across the NFL. On October 5, Randy had a big game against the Green Bay Packers in front of a huge television audience. He caught 5 passes for 190 yards and 2 touchdowns. Then, in a Thanksgiving Day game against the Dallas Cowboys, Randy caught 3 passes—all of them for touchdowns!

Randy congratulates Cris Carter after Carter's touchdown against the Carolina Panthers on November 19, 2000.

With 17 touchdowns, he set a new NFL record for touchdown receptions by a rookie and was named Rookie of the Year. He won almost every rookie award possible, was named All-Pro, and played in the Pro Bowl. Better yet, he helped the Vikings to a 15–1 record, the best record in the team's history.

RANDY MOSS TODAY

In 1999, his second season, Randy again put up big numbers. He set a new team record with 1,413 receiving yards. He caught 80 passes and scored 11 more touchdowns. He also returned a punt for a touchdown and even threw a touchdown pass to Cris Carter!

At the end of the season, Randy was selected to the Pro Bowl for the second straight year. In the NFL all-star game, Randy caught 9 passes for 212 yards and was named the game's Most Valuable Player.

In the 2000 season, Randy was again among the league's best receivers. He broke his team record for receiving yards with 1,477, and led the NFL in touchdown catches with 15. He was also selected to the Pro Bowl for the third straight year. Randy is one of the best players in the National Football League, and he has helped the Minnesota Vikings be one of the league's best teams. And when the quarterback throws the ball up high in Randy's direction, it's usually Randy who makes the catch.

Randy jumps into the stands as fans celebrate his touchdown against the Dallas Cowboys during the NFC Wild Card game on January 9, 2000.

TIMELINE

February 13, 1977	Randy Moss is born in Rand, West Virginia.
1993	Randy is named West Virginia's top high school basketball player.
1994	Randy is again named West Virginia's top high school basketball player and Football Player of the Year. He also leads DuPont to the West Virginia state football championship and accepts a scholarship to Notre Dame.
1995	After helping a friend in a fight, Randy is arrested, loses his scholarship to Notre Dame, and spends 30 days in jail. He agrees to attend Florida State University.
1996	Randy participates in spring practice at Florida State, is found to have taken drugs, loses his scholarship to Florida State, and spends 90 days in jail.
Fall 1996	Randy enrolls at Marshall University and leads its Thundering Herd to the Division 1-AA championship. He also ties Jerry Rice's record with 28 touchdown catches.
1997	Randy sets a new Division 1 record with 25 touchdown catches and wins the Biletnikoff Award as the nation's top receiver. He also finishes fourth in the Heisman Trophy voting and is named first-team All-American.
1998	In the 21st pick, Randy is drafted by the Minnesota Vikings. He scores 17 touchdowns to set a new record for rookie touchdown receptions, is named Rookie of the Year, and is named to the Pro Bowl.
1999	Randy sets a team record for receiving yards, is named to the Pro Bowl, and catches 11 more touchdown passes.
December 12, 2000	Randy is named to the Pro Bowl for the third straight year.

 Randy smiles from the sidelines after making a touchdown during an August 18, 2000 game against the Arizona Cardinals.　23

GLOSSARY

defensive back (dee-FEN-siv back)
A defensive back is a player on the defense who covers a wide receiver. Randy Moss is usually covered by two defensive backs.

draft (DRAFT)
In professional sports, the draft is the way in which teams choose new players. Randy Moss was selected 21st in the National Football League draft in 1998.

professional (pro-FESH-un-ull)
In sports, a professional is someone good enough to get paid rather than just playing for fun. Randy Moss always wanted to be a professional football player.

quarterback (KWOR-ter-bak)
The quarterback is the player on the offense who passes the ball to the wide receivers. Randy Moss helps his quarterback by making spectacular catches.

racism (RAY-sih-zim)
Racism is the belief that some people are better than others because of the color of their skin. Randy Moss battled racism when he was in high school.

scholarship (SKOL-er-ship)
A scholarship is a special award that pays for a student's schooling, sometimes in exchange for playing a sport. Randy Moss lost two scholarships because he got into trouble.

touchdown (TUTCH-down)
A touchdown is a way to score points in football by carrying the ball into the other team's end zone. Randy Moss scores many touchdowns.

training (TRAYN-ing)
In sports, training is working out to stay in good physical shape. Randy Moss goes into training with Cris Carter during the off-season.

wide receiver (WIDE ree-SEE-ver)
A wide receiver is a player on a football team who catches passes from the quarterback. Randy Moss is a wide receiver.

24

INDEX